YUMA COUNTY LIBRARY DISTRICT

Mortician

VIRGINIA LOH-HAGAN

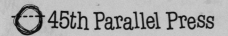

45th Parallel Press

Published in the United States of America by Cherry Lake Publishing
Ann Arbor, Michigan
www.cherrylakepublishing.com

Content Adviser: Jeffrey M. Jentzen, M.D., Ph.D., Professor, Department of Pathology, and Director, Autopsy and Forensic Services at the University of Michigan Health System
Reading Adviser: Marla Conn, ReadAbility, Inc.
Book Design: Felicia Macheske

Photo Credits: © LoloStock / Shutterstock.com, cover, 1; © TFoxFoto / Shutterstock.com, 5; © Dave Newman / Shutterstock.com, 6; © David Kay / Shutterstock.com, 9; © Photographee.eu / Shutterstock.com, 11; © Marcelmaaktfotoos / Dreamstime.com, 12; © Nordicphotos / Alamy, 14-15; © Kzenon / Shutterstock.com, 17; © Rich Legg / iStock, 19; © Tyler Olson / Dreamstime.com, 21; © Marzolino / Shutterstock.com, 23; © Brand X Pictures / Thinkstock, 25; © CaseyHillPhoto / iStock, 27; © ZUMA Press, Inc / Alamy, 28; © ARENA Creative / Shutterstock.com, cover and multiple interior pages; © oculo / Shutterstock.com, multiple interior pages; © Denniro / Shutterstock.com, multiple interior pages; © PhotoHouse / Shutterstock.com, multiple interior pages; © Miloje / Shutterstock.com, multiple interior pages

45th Parallel Press is an imprint of Cherry Lake Publishing.

Library of Congress Cataloging-in-Publication Data

Loh-Hagan, Virginia, author.
  Mortician / Virginia Loh-Hagan.
      pages cm. — (Odd jobs)
  Summary: "From the interesting and intriguing to the weird and wonderful, Mortician is HIGH interest combined with a LOW level of complexity to help struggling readers along. The carefully written, considerate text will hold readers' interest and allow for successful mastery, understanding, and enjoyment of reading about morticians. Clear, full-color photographs with captions provide additional accessible information. A table of contents, glossary with simplified pronunciations, and index all enhance achievement and comprehension."
— Provided by publisher.
  Includes bibliographical references and index.
  ISBN 978-1-63470-025-2 (hardcover) — ISBN 978-1-63470-052-8 (pbk.) — ISBN 978-1-63470-079-5 (pdf)
— ISBN 978-1-63470-106-8 (ebook)
 1. Undertakers and undertaking—Juvenile literature. 2. Vocational guidance. I. Title.

 RA622.L64 2016
 393—dc23
                    2015008262

Cherry Lake Publishing would like to acknowledge the work of The Partnership for 21st Century Skills.
Please visit *www.p21.org* for more information.

Printed in the United States of America
Corporate Graphics Inc.

Contents

Chapter 1
Heroes in the Shadows 4

Chapter 2
Working with Dead Bodies 8

Chapter 3
The Call to Be a Mortician 16

Chapter 4
Embalming 22

Chapter 5
Living and Laughing 26

Did You Know? 30
Consider This! 31
Learn More 31
Glossary 32
Index 32
About the Author 32

CHAPTER 1

Heroes in the Shadows

How do morticians help people at accidents? How are they heroes? Why and how did morticians in Chicago help stop city violence?

Think about plane crashes. Think about fires. Many people get hurt. Some people die.

Firefighters and policemen are there. They help save people. Morticians are there, too. They also help people.

Morticians handle dead bodies. They use **chemicals**, or special mixtures. The chemicals don't let bodies rot.

Family can see the bodies later. The chemicals also clean the bodies. This stops sicknesses from spreading.

Morticians are heroes. They take care of the **deceased**. The deceased are people who have died.

Morticians work alongside rescue workers.

Chicago is a city in the United States. Many young people there have been killed by guns. Morticians didn't like this. They did something about it.

More than 30 morticians worked together. They drove their **hearses**. Hearses are special cars for **coffins**. Coffins are boxes for dead bodies. They drove to where a student was shot to death. They wanted the killings to stop.

Hearses are sometimes called funeral coaches.
They are long and black.

Voice from the Field
CAITLIN DOUGHTY

Caitlin Doughty is a mortician. She lives in Los Angeles. She is the founder of The Order of the Good Death. This group helps people not be scared of death. She created a series on the Internet. It's called "Ask a Mortician." She answers people's questions. There is an episode called "It Gets Better, Morbid Kids!" She writes, "Here is a short video I did in response to the messages and emails I get from younger people who want to be morticians (or some other delightfully deathy career) but are told that they are deviant or creepy. WRONG. You are mortality explorers and big thinkers and don't let anyone tell you different. Our fear of death is a problem with society, not you." Watch the video at www.orderofthegooddeath.com/it-gets-better-morbid-kids#.VSyAFIctH4h.

Morticians don't benefit from such deaths. Dorothy Hudson is a mortician. She was in the event. She said, "We're burying too many of our young people." Morticians want people to live long lives.

CHAPTER 2

Working with Dead Bodies

What is a funeral? What do morticians do in order to prepare dead bodies and families for funerals? What is cremation? How do morticians respect dead bodies?

A mortician is a **funeral** director. A funeral is a service. It is a way to honor the deceased. Morticians help families. They plan funerals.

Morticians take care of dead bodies. They remove bodies from the place of death. They help families make decisions. Families decide what to do with the bodies.

Some people want to be **embalmed**. Embalming doesn't let bodies rot. Morticians use chemicals to do this.

There are different types of funerals.

Morticians have other tasks. **Dressing** means they dress the bodies in clothes. **Casketing** means they place the bodies in the casket. A casket is a coffin. **Cossetting** means they apply makeup. They want the deceased to look nice for the funeral.

Sometimes, morticians need to **restore**, or fix, bodies. They use clay, cotton, wax, or **plaster**. Plaster is a paste that hardens.

A person got shot in the chest. Mortician Jamie Reed fixed his body. She spent three days with him. She said, "I got attached to him." She felt close to him. Morticians care about people.

Morticians spend a lot of time preparing the deceased for the funeral.

Ashes can be scattered in the woods or in the ocean.

Some people want to be **cremated**. They want to be turned into ashes. Morticians take care of this. They burn bodies at high heat. It takes about three hours.

Ash is sandy. It is bumpy. Some people put ashes in urns. Urns are containers. Family members can keep the **urns**. They can bury the urns.

Some people want their ashes to be **scattered**. This means they throw the ashes. Family members scatter ashes in a special place.

Morticians respect dead bodies. They follow rules set by the National Funeral Directors Association. This is a group that manages morticians. Morticians have to show "the highest respect and dignity." Morticians treat dead bodies with honor.

Morticians properly care for bodies. They move bodies. They handle bodies. They make sure the bodies look comfortable. They make sure the bodies are covered.

It's a crime to harm dead bodies. People can go to jail.

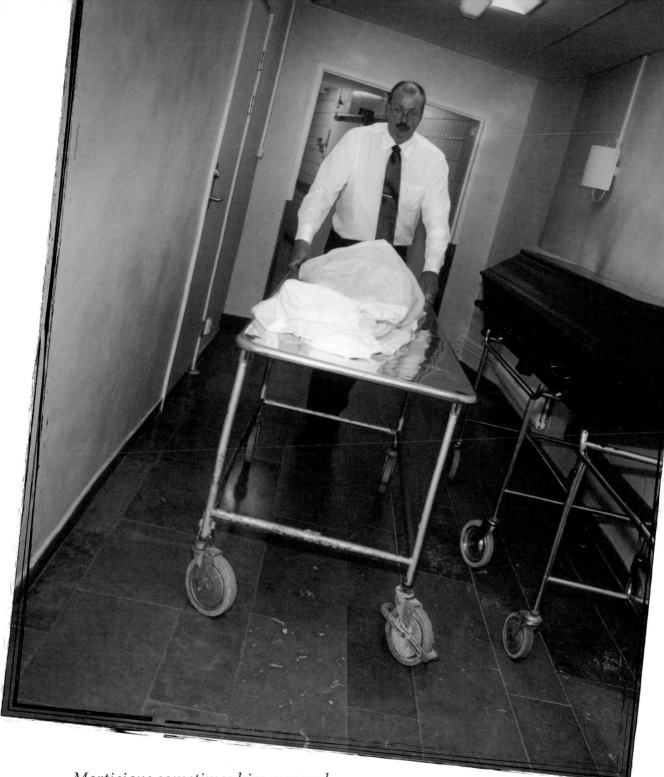

Morticians sometimes hire removal technicians to transport bodies.

CHAPTER 3

The Call to Be a Mortician

Why do people decide to be morticians? What do people need to do in order to become a mortician?

Morticians choose this odd job for several reasons. For many, it's a family business. There are six **generations** of morticians in Caleb Wilde's family. Wilde Funeral Home started in 1928. His grandfather embalmed his first body at age 6. Caleb played hide-and-seek. He ran among the coffins. He's been around funerals his whole life.

Carol Myers is also in the family business. Her funeral home started in 1904. More women are becoming morticians. She said, "We're here to help people get through their **grief**." Grief is pain and suffering. People are sad when their loved ones die. Myers thinks women can deal with emotions better than men.

Families run many funeral homes.

BRYAN FOSTER

Bryan Foster is the first African American mortician in Madison, Wisconsin. His funeral home is Foster Funeral and Cremation Service. He said, "I wanted to be in funeral services back in junior high." He embalmed deceased grasshoppers with Elmer's Glue. He made them little caskets. He made tissue paper flowers. He hosted fake funeral services. Today, he gives real funeral services. Foster is mentoring Dawn Adams. Adams is his apprentice. She wants to be the city's first female African American mortician. Foster wants to provide services to all people. But African Americans have special needs. They need morticians who know how to treat black skin and hair. Foster also helps plan services for Latino and Hmong families.

For others, being a mortician is a **calling**. A calling is a strong desire. Mike Parke has had good experiences with death. He faced death when he got sick. He dealt with his grandfather's death. He was 14 years old. Being a mortician was a "call to serve." He wants to honor the dead. He also wants to respect the wishes of the living.

Other people find the job interesting. Gina Krotee was inspired by a TV show. It was about a family of morticians. She stopped studying to be a wedding planner. She became a mortician instead. She said, "People can die in some really scary ways. … I focus on the body as a memory of their life."

Death can be sad. Morticians have a healthy outlook on death.

Morticians study mortuary science.

Each state has rules for becoming a mortician. Morticians have to be at least 21 years old. They need to pass state and national tests. They need to work as **apprentices**. Apprentices help morticians. They learn from morticians. Morticians train apprentices. They should have many years of experience.

Morticians also need some college education. They learn about funeral services. They learn about helping people with grief. They learn how to embalm. They need to get a special **license**, or permit, to embalm. They practice embalming on about 100 bodies.

CHAPTER 4

Embalming

What is the history of embalming? How does embalming work? What are the dangers of embalming?

Embalming became popular during the U.S. Civil War. Many men died. They died far from home. Family members wanted their bodies. So, people needed a new way to handle the dead bodies. Doctors embalmed the bodies. They did this on the battlefield. Then they sent the bodies home.

Abraham Lincoln was also embalmed. His body was put on a funeral train. It visited 444 communities in seven states.

Embalming schools soon opened. People learned how to embalm. Doctors were no longer needed. States required embalmers to have licenses. This created the funeral business. Death used to be handled at home. Now, morticians can take over.

Funerals used to be in people's homes.

Tattoo Artist
KNOW THE LINGO!

Bereaved: the immediate family of the deceased

Casket: coffin

Cooler: cold room for dead bodies

Coroner: an official who confirms death

Corpse: dead body

Cremains: the remains of a body after cremation

Crematory: building with the furnace, or oven

Exhume: digging up the remains after they've been buried

Memorial: ceremony remembering the deceased

Morgue: place where dead bodies wait to be identified

Obituary: notice of death in a newspaper

Refers: short for refrigerators where bodies are kept

Retort: crematory oven

Rigor mortis: when muscles stiffen after dying

Survivors: living people the deceased left behind

Viewing: opportunity to see the deceased before burial

Undertaker: another word for mortician

Wake: a watch kept over the deceased the night before the funeral

Morticians remove blood from the body. They use machines to push fluids into the body. They push blood out. Then they fill the body with chemicals. Embalming firms the skin. It **preserves** the body. Preserve means to keep it in its original state.

Embalming is not enjoyable. Morticians face problems. The chemicals can cause cancer. Cancer is a sickness. So they wear safety gear. They are also not well-respected. People think they smell like death. Morticians smell like chemicals. They don't smell like dead bodies.

Morticians provide a great service. They take care of our deceased.

Embalmers use a lot of chemicals. They use formaldehyde and embalming fluid.

CHAPTER 5

Living and Laughing

How much do morticians work? Why do morticians need to be calm and understanding? Why do morticians need to have a sense of humor?

Morticians might work 24 hours a day. They work weekends. They work holidays. Death happens at any time. Morticians have to embalm within 24 hours.

Morticians are calm. People need time to feel better. Morticians spend a lot of time with the family. They work more with the living than the dead.

Morticians are understanding. They know people get mad. Mortician Caitlin Doughty said, "They're angry that somebody has died. And they're looking for somebody to take it out on." Morticians help people.

Morticians wake up in the middle of the night. They have to take care of people.

Dealing with death can be sad. It's good to have a sense of humor. Morticians find things to laugh about. This helps them not be sad.

Ken McKenzie's father died. He was 12 years old. His father's mortician was funny. He said, "She was able to stop my grandmother and mother from arguing, and make me and 12 other kids laugh in 40 seconds. I wanted to do that."

McKenzie plans fun funerals. He planned a funeral for a race-car driver. It was at a car store. There was a crew. There was a race car. Two people waved red-and-

Morticians can get "compassion fatigue." They become tired from caring too much. It's good for them to laugh.

white flags. McKenzie uses special memories from the person's life.

Funerals are a celebration of life. Funny morticians help us remember that.

THAT HAPPENED?!?

Walter Williams died in his home. He lived in Mississippi. He was 78 years old. He had no pulse, or heartbeat. He was declared to be dead. He was put into a body bag. He was zipped up. He was taken to a funeral home. His body was in storage for a night. Something strange happened the next morning. Byron Porter was his mortician. He said, "We were getting ready to transport him to the embalming table in the embalming room, when we noticed he was moving." Williams kicked in the body bag. He was still alive! Two weeks later, Williams died for real.

DID YOU KNOW?

- Dangerous things can happen in crematory ovens. Morticians have to check bodies. They have to remove machines like pacemakers. These can explode in the oven. Morticians also have to be careful with overweight people. The extra fat can start a fire in the ovens. This could burn down the funeral home.

- People used to keep dead bodies at home. They put dry ice around the body. The body is good for a couple of days. Then the body starts to rot.

- The Latham family live in Arkansas. During the day, they are morticians. At night, they are wrestlers. LaFonce Latham is "Big Daddy." They're featured in a reality show. It is called *Wrestling with Death*.

- James Lowry is a mortician in West Virginia. He collects coffins and funeral antiques. He shared them at a horror and science fiction meeting. He's been collecting for 25 years.

- People can't just scatter ashes anywhere. There are rules. A man scattered his mother's ashes in a football stadium. He ran into the stadium during a game. His mother was a big Philadelphia Eagles fan. He was arrested.

- Jeff Friedman created a mobile funeral home. This is a mortuary on wheels. He brings the funeral business to people's doorsteps. Morticians are getting creative about their job.

CONSIDER THIS!

TAKE A POSITION! Manitou Springs, Colorado, has hosted coffin races. They've done this since 1995. It takes place around Halloween. It starts with a parade of coffins and hearses. People wear costumes. People decorate a coffin. They turn it into a race car. Many morticians support this event. Do you think there should be "fun" in "funerals"? Is it okay to joke about funerals and death? Argue your point with reasons and evidence.

SAY WHAT? Cultures have different beliefs about death. Some families have a hard time finding a mortician. They have to find other ways to honor their cultural traditions. Not all morticians will provide special services. Learn about how another culture handles death. Explain this culture's traditions and beliefs about death.

THINK ABOUT IT! There are many stories about zombies and vampires. People find the undead interesting. But real death makes many people uncomfortable. Some people think it is morbid, or disturbing, to discuss death. What do you think about this?

SEE A DIFFERENT SIDE! Some people don't believe in burials. They think it's unfriendly to the environment. Some morticians are promoting a "green cemetery." This means no embalming and no coffins. People would be placed straight into the ground. They'll be wrapped in a cloth. What do you think about the funeral business "going green"?

LEARN MORE

PRIMARY SOURCES
Funeral Director: Making a Living Dealing with the Dead, a documentary about the business of death (2013).

SECONDARY SOURCES
Colman, Penny. *Corpses, Coffins, and Crypts: A History of Burial.* New York: Henry Holt and Company, 1997.
Griffey, Harriet. *Secrets of the Mummies.* London; New York: DK Publishing, 2013.
Mundy, Michaelene, and R.W. Alley (illustrator). *What Happens When Someone Dies? A Child's Guide to Death and Funerals.* St. Meinrad, IN: Abbey Press, 2009

WEB SITES
International Cemetery, Cremation and Funeral Association: https://www.iccfa.com
National Funeral Directors Association: http://nfda.org
National Funeral Directors and Morticians Association: www.nfdma.com

GLOSSARY

apprentice (uh-PREN-tis) someone who trains under an expert to learn the job

calling (KAWL-ing) a strong desire

casketing (KAS-ket-ing) when morticians place the bodies in the casket

chemicals (KEM-i-kuhlz) special mixtures

coffins (KAW-finz) boxes for dead bodies

cossetting (KA-set-ting) when morticians apply makeup to dead bodies

cremated (KREE-mate-id) body burned to ashes

deceased (dih-SEEST) people who have died

dressing (DRES-ing) when morticians dress the dead bodies in clothes

embalmed (em-BAHMD) a dead body preserved with chemicals to prevent the body from rotting

funeral (FYOO-nur-uhl) a special service or memorial for the deceased

generations (jen-uh-RAY-shuhnz) the amount of time between the birth of parents and the birth of their children

grief (GREEF) sadness from loss, sorrow, pain, or suffering

hearses (HURS-ez) special cars that carry coffins

license (LYE-suhns) a permit

plaster (PLAS-tur) paste that hardens

preserve (pri-ZURV) to keep something in its original state

restore (rih-STOR) fix or reshape

scattered (SKAT-urd) thrown around

urns (URNZ) containers for ashes

INDEX

apprentices, 21
ashes, 12, 13, 30

casketing, 10
chemicals, 4–5, 9, 25
coffins, 6, 10, 30
cossetting, 10

cremation, 13, 30

deceased, 5, 8, 11
dressing, 10

education, 21
embalming, 9, 21, 22–25, 26

funerals, 8, 9, 11, 23, 28–29, 30

grief, 17

hearses, 6

lingo, 24

morticians, 4–7
    challenges, 25, 26–29
    how to become one, 16–21
    reasons for choosing job, 16–19
    what they do, 8–15
mortuary science, 20

respect, 14, 18

sense of humor, 28

ABOUT THE AUTHOR

Dr. Virginia Loh-Hagan is an author, university professor, former classroom teacher, and curriculum designer. She celebrates life every day. She lives in San Diego with her very tall husband and very naughty dogs. To learn more about her, visit www.virginialoh.com.